The Pause

Finding the Small Space Between What Happens and What You Do Emotional Regulation for Women

Michael J. Rogers Ph.D.

Mind-Full

Mind-Full Publishing

Contents

The Pause

Finding the Small Space Between What Happens and What You Do

Emotional Regulation for Women

Michael J. Rogers, Ph.D.

A Note Before You Begin

This book is a companion for everyday emotional life, and it is written by a mental-health professional as a set of tools and reflections, not as therapy or medical advice. It is not a substitute for care from a qualified professional.

If you are struggling with trauma, or with thoughts of harming yourself, or with a relationship in which you do not feel safe, please reach out to a licensed clinician or a crisis line in your area. The pause is a tool for the ordinary hard moments of a life. It was never meant to help anyone endure harm.

The scenes in these pages are composites, drawn from common human experience and shaped to protect the privacy of real people. Any resemblance to a particular person is unintended.

A Little Extra Help Along the Way

As you read *The Pause*, you may want something simple to keep nearby to help you put these ideas into practice. I've created a free companion resource with practical exercises from the book, including a Personal Pain Wheel and tools for creating your own Pause Plan.

To receive your free copy, follow the QR code:

Put **"The Pause Resources"** in the subject line, and I'll send them to you. I enjoy hearing from readers and learning how you're putting the pause into practice.

Michael J. Rogers, Ph.D.

Introduction

It's a little after three in the morning, and you're awake again.

Not because of a noise, the baby, or the dog. You're awake because of a sentence. Something you said at dinner, something you didn't say, or the tone that came out when your daughter asked for one more thing. You heard your own voice go sharp and thin, and even as it was happening, you couldn't seem to stop it.

You've been lying there replaying it for the better part of an hour. The room is dark and quiet, but inside your chest there's a low hum that won't settle. It's like a soda bottle that's been shaken and put back on the shelf. Everything looks still from the outside, but underneath, there's pressure.

You're a careful person, and that's part of what makes three in the morning so lonely. You care, probably too much sometimes, about how you affect the people around you. You read the books. You know the language. You've told yourself a hundred times, Tomorrow I'll be calmer. Tomorrow I'll be more patient. Tomorrow I'll pause instead of snapping.

Then tomorrow comes with all its noise and speed, and somewhere between the alarm and the front door, the old reaction shows up again. By nine in the morning, you're already apologizing, or wishing you could.

I want to tell you something before we do any work at all, because I think you may have been carrying the opposite belief for a long time. Those moments don't mean there's something fundamentally wrong with you. They don't prove that you're too sensitive, too much, or privately broken in some way you hope nobody notices.

There's a reason your reactions happen so quickly. There's a reason the heat arrives before the thought, and your mind starts telling a story before you've even caught your breath. Those reactions were built. They came from a body doing one of its oldest jobs. They were shaped by things that happened before you had much said in them, by love and fear and a hundred quiet lessons about who you needed to be to feel safe and wanted. That matters, because something that was built can be understood. Once you understand the pattern, you can begin to change it.

Let me also tell you what I'm not going to ask you to do. I'm not going to ask you to become a different kind of person. You don't need to trade in your sensitivity or turn yourself into someone breezy and unbothered who lets everything roll off. That person isn't better than you, and honestly, she probably exists mostly on the internet. The passion, depth, and caring that sometimes overwhelm you are also part of what makes you good at loving people. I have no interest in taking those things away from you.

This book asks for something much smaller and much more doable than a personality transplant.

It asks you to get better at one moment.

There's a space, very small at first, between what happens and what you do next. Someone makes a sharp comment, and there's a flicker before you fire back. Your child melts down in the cereal aisle, and there's a sliver of time before your voice rises. Your phone lights up with that name, and for half a second, before your thumbs start moving, there's a gap.

Most of us were never taught that the gap is there. Even fewer were taught that it can grow. With practice, the flicker can become a breath, and the breath can become a choice. That gap is where your power has been hiding all along. This book is about finding it and learning to live there, one ordinary moment at a time.

Along the way, I'm going to show you a few things that took me years to understand while sitting with people during some of the hardest seasons of their lives. We'll look at how suffering works and how easily we add to pain that was already heavy enough. I'll show you a pattern I call the Pain Wheel, the loop running underneath so many of our worst moments, and how recognizing that loop gives us a chance to step out of it.

I'll show you what actually belongs inside the pause once you find it. It comes down to two things, the only two things that were ever truly yours to govern: what you do and how you hold what's happening to you. Your actions and your attitudes. Everything else, the other person, the past, the outcome, is on the other side of a line you were never able to cross anyway.

The work in these pages is meant for real life, which means it has to work in a busy one. You won't need an hour of silence, a cushion, or a free weekend. These practices are small enough to use in the car, in the bathroom with the door locked while someone is knocking, or in the ten seconds between a text arriving and your response going out.

Some take a single breath.

That's intentional. A tool that only works when life is calm isn't much of a tool, because the moments that undo us rarely wait for calm.

I also want to be clear about what this book can and can't do, because I think you've probably been handed enough promises already. It won't cure you. There's no formula here, and you're not going to reach a point where you're never triggered again. Anyone promising that is selling something. What I'm offering is a skill.

It's more like learning an instrument. At first, it's slow and awkward. Then, with practice, more of it begins to happen naturally. You'll find the pause, lose it, and find it again. Some days you'll catch the moment and feel a small, private astonishment at the choice you didn't know you had. Other days you'll blow right past it and realize what happened at three in the morning. Both days belong to the same process. Even noticing too late means the muscle is beginning to work.

So, treat what follows as an experiment, not a test. There's no passing or failing here. There's no version of you who finishes the book successfully and another who flunks it. The old patterns will come back. When they do, that doesn't mean the experiment failed. The pattern is simply showing you where it still lives, which tells you where to bring the next small pause.

A few practical things before we begin. It'll help to read the early chapters in order because each one gives you something the next chapter will build on. Later, once you understand the shape of the work, come back to whatever chapter fits the week you're having. Go to boundaries when a request has you cornered. Go to parenting when bedtime has become a battlefield.

Keep something nearby to write in too, whether it's a notebook or the Notes app on your phone. A lot of this work happens on the page, where a racing thought can finally slow down enough to be examined. And go gently. Pick one or two practices at a time. Trying to do everything at once creates its own kind of pressure, and pressure is exactly what we're here to let out of the bottle.

You've been awake at three in the morning long enough. Let me show you the small space where the mornings begin to change.

Chapter One

Chapter 1: The Small Space That Changes Everything

Think back over the last week and try to find a completely neutral Tuesday afternoon, just an ordinary hour when nothing happened and nothing much stirred in you. You probably can't.

What you can remember are the moments that caught fire. The argument in the kitchen. The tears you held back in the school pickup line. The smile you wore at work while something sour was building underneath it. The door your child slammed, maybe in a way that sounded uncomfortably familiar. The neutral hours disappear. The reactive ones stay with us, stored in detail and ready to replay at three in the morning.

From the inside, life can start to feel like one long sequence of things happening to you and you reacting before you even understand what you're feeling. Something lands, and you're already snapping, shrinking, defending, explaining. Only afterward does the feeling catch up and tell you what was going on.

That's part of what makes reactions feel so uncontrollable. It's hard to steer something you didn't see coming. If you slow one of those moments down, almost like watching a film frame by frame, something appears that you usually miss. Between what happens and what you do next, there's a small space. Sometimes it's only half a second. Nobody may have ever pointed it out to you, but it's been there in every reactive moment you've ever had. That little space is what this book is about, because it's the one place in the whole sequence where you still have a choice.

From "Life Happens" to "I React"

You probably know the feeling I'm describing. It's like being on a conveyor belt. The day starts and you're already behind.

You're carrying more than you have hands for, and before you can put one thing down, something else gets handed to you.

An email opens with a sentence that tightens your chest. Your partner sighs in a certain way, and before he's said a word, you can feel your body change. One of the kids uses that tone, and suddenly your own voice comes out louder and sharper than you meant it to.

Then comes the second wave. Maybe an hour later. Maybe that night. The replay. The embarrassment. The shame. The quiet conclusion that you're doing all of this wrong.

For a long time, you may have treated those moments as evidence about your character. I want to loosen that belief a little, because it isn't fair and it isn't accurate. The speed is real, but it isn't a moral failure.

Your nervous system is built to move faster than conscious thought. It's constantly scanning the room, the people in it, the tone of a voice, the look on a face, for anything that resembles something your body learned to treat as danger. When it finds a match, it can sound the alarm before the thinking part of your brain has even joined the conversation.

It's more like a smoke detector than a wise advisor. A smoke detector doesn't stop to ask whether the smoke is coming from a burning house or a steak in a hot pan. It screams first. Evolution decided a thousand false alarms were worth it if one of them caught the real fire.

So, when you react before you've had time to think, it doesn't mean you're weak. It means you're fast in exactly the way your body was designed to be fast. Somewhere along the way, it learned which tones, faces, silences, and situations meant trouble, and it practiced its response until that response barely needed your permission anymore. But living at the mercy of that alarm has a cost.

It can look like walking on eggshells in your own home because you're constantly trying to manage everybody else's mood before it becomes your problem. It can mean apologizing for things that didn't require an apology or saying yes when everything in you wanted to say no. It can wear down your sleep, your health, your concentration, and your confidence.

Over time, it can leave you with a private belief that you're somehow too much for the people you love, and that if they could really see all the pressure inside you, they'd eventually leave. That's a heavy belief to carry.

The Reason Insight Was Never Enough

Here's what may be most frustrating: you probably already understand a lot of this. Maybe you've been to therapy. Maybe you've read the books. Maybe you've spent long nights tracing your reactions back through your history until you can explain exactly why criticism gets to you, where the people-pleasing came from, and why certain situations light you up so quickly. Yet knowing all of that doesn't always help when the moment actually arrives. You can understand why you react and still react exactly the same way. Sometimes the only difference is that now you feel worse afterward because you think you should know better.

That's the gap this book is trying to close. The gap between understanding the reaction and knowing what to do in the half second before it takes over. Insight can show you the pattern. It doesn't automatically stop the pattern. What you've been missing isn't more self-criticism and probably isn't more explanation either. You need somewhere to stand and something small to do once you're there. That place is the pause.

The Gap You Already Use

Here's the good news: you already know how to pause. You do it all day long in situations that feel safe. You check the recipe before adding more salt. You glance in the mirror before leaving the house. You reread an email before hitting send and catch the sentence that sounds sharper than you intended. In each case, you put a small check between the impulse and the action.

So, you're not starting from zero. You're not someone who can't pause. You've simply never learned to bring that same skill into the emotional parts of your life, especially the rooms where the stakes feel highest and everything moves faster. That's the project in one sentence. You already know how to pause over a hot stove. Now you're going to learn how to pause over a hot feeling.

What Lives Inside the Pause

When you find that gap and manage to hold it open, even briefly, you discover that it isn't empty. There are two things inside it that belong to you. The first is your actions. You can choose what you say, what you don't say, how loudly you speak, whether you send the text now or tomorrow, whether you stay in the room or step away for five minutes. The second is your attitude. That's the inner posture you bring to the moment. Do you treat this as a catastrophe or an inconvenience? Do you turn against yourself, or do you stay on your own side while you deal with what happened?

Those two things, your actions and your attitudes, are yours. What isn't yours matters just as much. You can't use the pause to control the other person. You can't undo what already happened. You can't rewrite your childhood or erase the experiences that taught your body to react the way it does. You can't remove every pressure from your week.

We spend enormous amounts of energy trying to control those things anyway, then wonder why we're exhausted. The pause isn't where you fix your husband or rewrite your mother. It's simply the small piece of ground that actually belongs to you. Pausing doesn't mean swallowing your feelings or pretending to be calm. The feeling gets to be there. The pause only gives you a chance to decide what you're going to build on top of it. That's where your choice begins.

Pain, and the Suffering We Add

That brings us to one of the most important distinctions in this book: the difference between pain and the suffering we build on top of it. Pain is what happens first. The harsh comment hurts. The public tantrum floods you with embarrassment and helplessness. Rejection can feel almost physical because, to a nervous system built for belonging, it is. You don't choose that first layer. And nothing in this book is going to ask you to pretend it doesn't hurt.

Suffering is what often comes next. The comment hurts for thirty seconds, but then you replay it for three days. You decide what it means about you. You rehearse what you should have said. You punish yourself for caring. The tantrum ends, but afterward you decide you're a terrible mother who's damaging her children. That's the second layer.

The pain was handed to you. The suffering is what gets built on top of it, one floor at a time. I don't say that to blame you. Most of us build those floors without realizing we're doing it. Anything you're building is also something you can learn to stop building. The pause is where you begin to notice that you're holding the trowel.

Meet the Pain Wheel

I have a name for the loop that keeps all of this going. I call it the Pain Wheel.

It starts with *Pain*. Maybe loneliness, rejection, shame, exhaustion, or some ache that's been building for a while. Eventually you reach a point where you don't want to feel it anymore and you might say to yourself, *I can't take one more thing.* We will call this stop on the wheel *Hit Bottom.* When you are in a place where you feel like you can't tale one more thing, you start searching for a way to make the pain stop. We will call this part of the wheel Seek Relief. That when you reach for a *Behavior.*

Maybe you snap. Maybe you scroll. Maybe you pour another drink. Maybe you start fixing everybody else's problems. Maybe you say yes when you mean no. This becomes your go-to strategy to eliminate *Pain.* For a moment, it works. That's why the pattern is so powerful. The behavior actually does relieve the pressure, at least briefly. This is the part of the wheel we call *Feel Good.*

Then the *Consequence* arrives. The shame. The silence. The conflict. The exhaustion. The regret. Each *Consequence* creates a compounding effect on the *Pain,* which starts circling the Pain Wheel again.

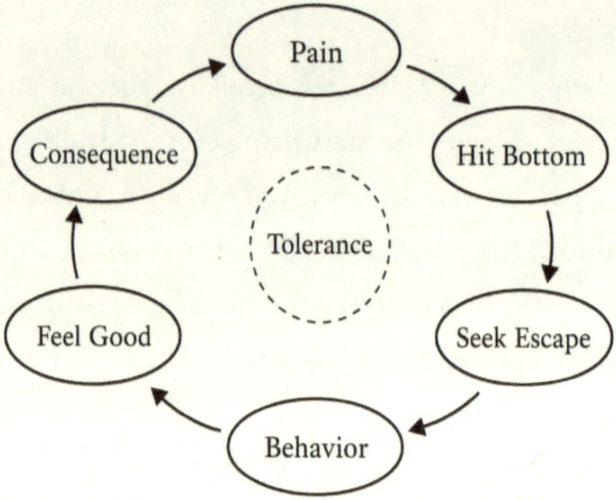

The Pain Wheel

At the center of the wheel is something I call *Tolerance*. Over time, the same behavior usually gives you less relief, so you need more of it. More scrolling. More sharpness. More disappearing. More control. The pain of the wheel doesn't stay the same size. It slowly compounds. That's one reason the pattern you're dealing with now may feel heavier than it did five years ago.

You can't stop the pain that starts the wheel. But you can learn to see the wheel turning. There's one place where you can reach in before the behavior takes over. That place is the pause.

It sits between the pain and the response. Everything else in this book is really about learning how to find that small space and stay there long enough to choose.

A First Practice

For now, don't try to fix anything, just start noticing. Once a day, catch yourself using an ordinary pause you already know how to use. Notice yourself rereading the message before sending it. Checking the mirror.

When you catch yourself doing it, say quietly to yourself: There it is. That's a pause. That's the skill. You don't need to use it in the hard moments yet. For now, you're simply learning to recognize something you've been doing all along. Later, we'll carry that same skill into the rooms where the feelings run hotter and the stakes feel higher. When we do, it starts becoming something that was yours already.

Chapter Two

Chapter 2: Why You React the Way You Do

Imagine you could open yourself up the way you open the back of an old watch and see what's happening inside during a hard conversation. It might feel like chaos from where you're sitting, but that's not what you'd see. You'd see a system at work, with each part doing a job it learned a long time ago. Your heart speeds up to move blood to your muscles. Your breathing gets shorter. Old voices start offering quick opinions about what this means and what you'd better do about it. Somewhere underneath all of that, a younger version of you recognizes the feeling and begins to stir.

None of it is random, and none of it means you're broken. Your reactions have been stitched together from your body, your history, and your relationships, all working faster than you can consciously think and trying, in their own ways, to keep you safe. If you want to change what comes out of you in those moments, it helps to understand what's happening inside you first. So, let's take a look at the works.

Your Body Has Three Basic Gears

Underneath many of your reactions is a nervous system that operates in a surprisingly small number of basic states. Once you begin to recognize which one you're in, a lot of what used to seem mysterious starts making more sense.

The first gear is the revved-up one. You're wired, buzzing, ready to do something. It may show up as anger or anxiety, or as the frantic feeling that something has to be fixed right now. Your body has decided there's a threat and has given you the fuel to fight it or get away from it.

The second gear is at the other end. When something feels too big to fight or escape, your system may shut things down instead. You go numb or foggy. You get tired. Maybe you become strangely calm, quiet, agreeable, or absent. Instead of fighting, you want the whole thing to end. You may find yourself saying yes just to make that happen.

Between those two is the gear you're looking for. It's the steady place where you can feel something strongly and still think at the same time. You're still present. You haven't stopped caring, and the feeling hasn't disappeared. You simply have enough of yourself available to make a choice.

Most of us spend less time there than we'd like. In a difficult conversation, we can even bounce between revved up and shut down several times. The important thing to remember is that none of these gears describes who you are. They're states, and states change. The pause gives you a small lever of your own, so when your body shifts into a gear you didn't choose, you can begin finding your way back toward steady.

The Alarm and the Thermostat

I mentioned the smoke detector in the last chapter, and it's worth staying with that image because it explains so much about the feeling of being hijacked by your own reactions. A smoke detector has one move. It doesn't stop to assess the situation or distinguish between a house fire and a piece of toast you left in too long. It senses smoke and starts screaming. That's exactly what you want when the house is actually on fire, but it can be pretty annoying when breakfast is the only thing in danger.

A lot of our reactivity works the same way. The alarm was tuned by earlier experiences to notice certain cues, and when something in the present resembles something from the past, it can go off at full volume even when nothing is actually burning.

A thermostat works differently. It notices that something has changed, makes an adjustment, and brings the room back toward balance. It responds rather than simply reacts. That's part of what you're learning to develop here. You're not trying to rip the smoke detector off the ceiling. Sometimes there really is a fire, and you need the alarm. You're learning to notice when it goes off and give yourself enough time to ask whether you're dealing with a fire or just the toast.

Why the Body Reacts to Things the Mind Has Forgotten

You've probably had reactions that seemed much bigger than the thing that caused them. A small criticism produces an enormous wave of emotion. A certain tone from your partner sends you straight into shutdown. You may even know while it's happening that your response seems out of proportion and still be unable to stop it.

Part of the reason is that the body remembers things the conscious mind may not be thinking about anymore. When something frightened or hurt you, especially if it happened early or often, your system learned what came with it. It noticed the volume of a voice, a certain look on a face, the particular quality of a silence. Those things became signals.

Years later, when something similar happens, your body may react to the whole history rather than only to what's happening now. The present moment strikes the match, but there may be years of accumulated fuel behind the reaction. Seen that way, some of your biggest reactions make more sense. They're often old attempts to keep an old pain from happening again.

This is why the sensations in your body can be treated as information without being treated as instructions. A tight throat and racing heart are telling you that your system senses danger. That information matters, but it isn't proof that you're actually in danger or that the person standing in front of you is the person who hurt you before. Part of learning to pause is being able to hear the alarm without immediately obeying it.

Your Inner Cast of Characters

There's another layer to this, and it helps explain why you can sometimes feel like several different versions of yourself in the course of a single day.

There's the competent version who handles things at work without much trouble. There may be an anxious version who shows up when a relationship feels uncertain. There's the one who loses patience with the kids and later wonders where that reaction came from. Maybe there's another who goes cold and silent when things get too intense.

These aren't necessarily masks, and they don't mean you're fake or fractured. Think of them instead as familiar patterns of thinking, feeling, and behaving that developed for a reason. Many of them learned their jobs because, at some point, those jobs helped protect you.

Even the inner critic can be understood this way. It gets to you first, pointing out everything you've done wrong before somebody else has the chance. Somewhere underneath that criticism is the idea that if you can find and fix every flaw yourself, maybe nobody else can use it against you. The pleaser works from a similar place, watching faces for signs of disappointment and trying to smooth things over before anyone pulls away. The controller, the fixer, even the person who cracks a joke the instant a room gets uncomfortable can all be trying to do the same basic thing: get ahead of pain before it arrives.

Usually, those protective reactions are guarding something more tender underneath. There may still be old shame there, fear of rejection, or the ache of not feeling chosen. Anything in the present that resembles those older wounds can wake the protectors up quickly. They aren't trying to ruin your marriage or your evening. They're using the tools they know to keep something painful from happening again.

The pause isn't about getting rid of those parts of yourself. It gives you enough room that the fastest and most frightened part doesn't automatically get to make the decision.

There's also a steadier version of you underneath all that noise, the part that can notice what's happening with some curiosity instead of immediately reacting to it. In a difficult moment, that part can seem very far away, but it hasn't disappeared. The pause gives it time to catch up. Each time you hold that gap open, even briefly, you give the steadier part of yourself a chance to decide what happens next.

The Invisible Rules You Live By

There's one more piece inside the works, and it may be the hardest to notice because it usually runs silently in the background.

Over time, messages we hear and experiences we have can harden into rules. Don't be a burden. Nice girls don't get angry. If everyone around me is happy, I'm safe. If somebody is unhappy, it's my job to fix it. Rest has to be earned. You may never have deliberately chosen any of those rules. You might even disagree with them if somebody said them out loud. But a rule doesn't have to be consciously believed to influence the way you live. It can quietly determine which feelings you allow yourself to have, what you apologize for, how much space you take up, and how responsible you feel for everybody else in the room.

Under those rules are often a few even simpler beliefs: I'm too much. I'm not enough. I'm only safe when everyone is pleased with me. They can feel like facts because they've been around for so long, but familiarity isn't the same thing as truth.

One of the most damaging things these beliefs do is turn an event into an identity. Something goes badly, and before you know it, that went badly has become I'm bad. One difficult exchange with your child becomes evidence that you're a bad mother. One mistake at work becomes proof that you're a fraud and eventually everyone will figure it out.

That small jump from what happened to who you are can turn an ordinary painful moment into something much heavier. Now you're not just dealing with the mistake or the argument. You're defending your whole sense of yourself.

The pause gives you a chance to catch that story while it's still being written. You can notice your mind reaching for the old conclusion and decide not to accept it automatically. That doesn't mean pretending the hard thing didn't happen. It means giving yourself enough time to consider whether the first interpretation your frightened mind offered is actually the truest one.

A Practice for This Chapter

For the next week, try becoming a quiet observer of your own gears. Don't worry about changing them yet. For now, you're just learning what they feel like. A few times during the day, ask yourself, Which gear am I in right now? Am I revved up, shut down, or steady? Don't judge the answer or immediately try to move yourself somewhere else. Just notice it the way you'd notice the weather.

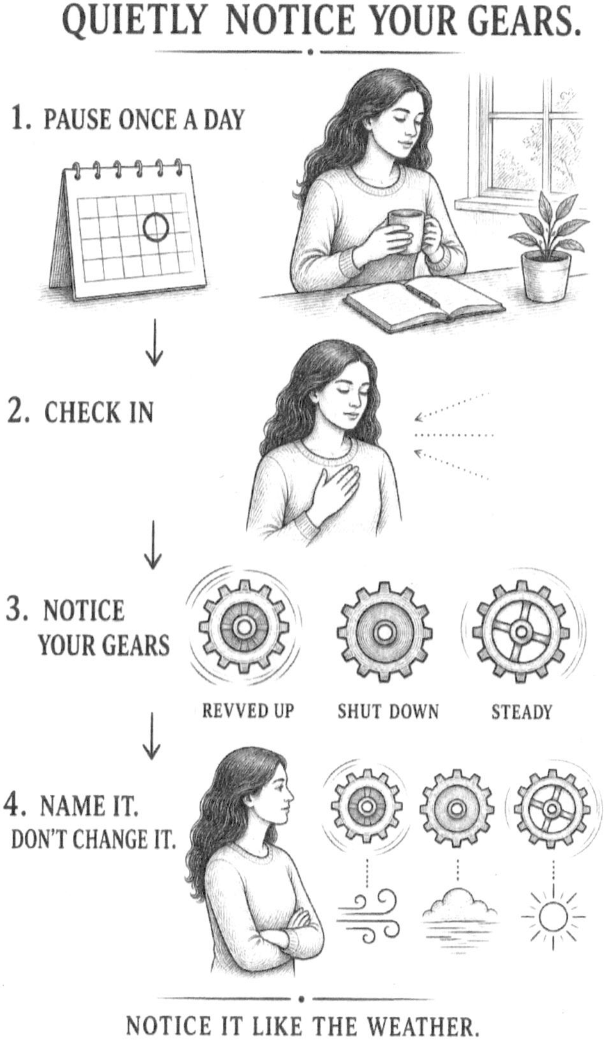
QUIETLY NOTICE YOUR GEARS.
1. PAUSE ONCE A DAY
2. CHECK IN
3. NOTICE YOUR GEARS
REVVED UP
SHUT DOWN
STEADY
4. NAME IT. DON'T CHANGE IT.
NOTICE IT LIKE THE WEATHER.

Which Gear?

After a few days, you may start catching the shifts themselves. You'll notice the fog beginning when a certain email arrives or feel yourself revving up when a particular name appears on your phone. That awareness matters more than it may seem. You can't make a choice about a state you don't realize you're entering.

First, learn to feel the gears change. In the chapters ahead, we'll work on what to do once you feel your hand reaching for the lever.

Chapter Three

Chapter 3: Mapping Your Personal Pain Wheel

Suppose someone followed you around for a week with a camera, not to catch you doing anything wrong, but simply to understand you. Watching the footage afterward, you'd probably notice something that's hard to see while you're living it. The same scenes keep coming back. The same tightening in your chest when someone uses a certain tone. The same clipped "it's fine" when it clearly isn't. The same quiet shutting down just before you hear yourself say yes to something you didn't want to do.

From the inside, those moments feel like ambushes. Each one seems to come out of nowhere. But from the outside, they would look more like intersections you've driven through before. The scenery changes, but the turn is familiar. That shift, from seeing the moment as an ambush to seeing it as an intersection, is what this chapter is about. An ambush gives you no choice. An intersection, once you recognize it, gives you somewhere to turn.

This week, you're going to begin mapping those intersections. Not with judgment, and not with the idea that you should've figured them out by now. You're simply going to bring them into the light. A great deal of their power comes from the fact that they happen so quickly and so automatically that you never get a good look at them. Once you can see the pattern on a page, it has already lost a little of its ability to run you.

Look for the Repeats

Start small. Don't go looking for the biggest explosion you've ever had. Those moments may be memorable, but they don't happen often enough to practice with. The better material is the ordinary friction that keeps showing up: the sharp reply in the car, the spiral after a friend takes too long to text back, the sick feeling when a coworker corrects you in front of other people.

Think of the last five times you felt flooded, ashamed, cornered, or out of control. Write each one down in a sentence or two, as plainly as you can. Try to describe what a camera would've seen rather than what your mind concluded about it. Then look across the five and ask what they have in common. Strip away the details of who was there and where it happened. What was the tender spot underneath? Were you being criticized? Ignored? Needed beyond what you had left to give? Controlled? Left out? Disappointed?

Most of us aren't running twenty different patterns. We're running a few familiar ones in different clothing. You may notice that several of your examples fall into the same general family. Criticism and rejection can be triggered by an eye roll, a correction, or a silence you interpret as disapproval. Conflict may show up when someone raises a voice or simply makes it clear they're unhappy with you. Disappointment appears when something you were counting on falls through. Chaos and uncertainty can come alive when plans change suddenly or the ground feels less stable than you expected. Neediness can be activated when someone keeps asking after you've already reached your limit.

Pay attention to what happens in your body as you read those possibilities. Sometimes your body recognizes the pattern before your mind is willing to name it. From what you find, choose your top three. Pick them because they happen often or because they hit hard, not because they seem like the "right" things to work on. Then give each one a short name that you'll recognize quickly.

One woman I think of called hers "Invisible," "Not Enough," and "Losing Control." Once she had names for them, something changed. She could feel the old reaction beginning and think, Oh, this is Invisible again. That tiny bit of recognition gave her a little distance from the reaction, and that distance became the beginning of a choice. Your three names can work the same way. They become early warning lights. When one of them comes on, you know the Pain Wheel may be starting to turn.

There's one thing to watch for while you do this. Naming your patterns can wake up shame. You may hear an old voice saying that a healthier person wouldn't have these reactions at all. Don't trust that voice. Everyone has tender places, and learning where yours are isn't an indictment. It's information.

If the exercise starts feeling heavy, stop. Get some water. Walk around. Come back later. You're not trying to force a breakthrough. You're learning something true about yourself, and you can learn it without treating yourself harshly.

Slow One Scene Down

Once you've identified your themes, choose one recent incident attached to one of them. Pick something manageable. You're going to replay it slowly on the page, almost frame by frame, and walk it around the Pain Wheel.

Start with what actually happened. Keep this part as clean as you can. Instead of writing, "He dismissed me and made me feel small," write, "He looked at his phone while I was talking and said, 'mm-hm.'" A camera could've recorded the phone and the sound he made. It couldn't have recorded "dismissive." That part came later. The distinction matters because much of the work ahead depends on separating the event from the meaning your mind added to it.

Next, go to the body. What happened there before you had a clear thought? Maybe your throat tightened. Maybe heat climbed your neck. Your stomach dropped. Your head felt light. Your chest tightened. Even if the sensation seems minor, write it down. Those small physical changes are often the first sign that the wheel has started moving.

Then listen for the thoughts that followed. What did your mind immediately decide the moment meant? Write the words the way they actually came, even if they sound exaggerated now. He doesn't care what I think. I'm boring. Nobody listens to me. I always do this.

Those thoughts matter because this is where the pain begins gathering a story. The event happened, the body reacted, and then the mind rushed in to explain what it all meant. That explanation is often where the suffering starts to grow.

Now write down what you did next. Include the obvious things and the quiet ones. What did you say? What tone did you use? Did you leave the room, go silent, send the text, apologize too quickly, start cleaning, begin scrolling, or reach for something to eat even though you weren't hungry? Even though it may feel like a confession, it's just taking inventory.

Finally, follow the scene into the aftermath. What happened in the next few hours or days? Did resentment stay with you? Shame? Sadness? Did you replay the scene in bed that night? Did the fallout create more of the same pain you started with?

That's the circle of the Pain Wheel. The behavior gives you some kind of relief or release, but the consequence often brings you right back to the original pain, sometimes with a little more weight added. Once you can see the whole loop on paper, something important becomes visible. There's usually one place where a pause could make the biggest difference, and it's near the top of the wheel, after the first signal from the body but before the behavior takes over.

Find the Pauses You Already Have

Now look for the other side of the map. Your week wasn't made entirely of reactions. There were moments when you almost reacted and didn't. Maybe you started to snap and softened your voice. Maybe you typed the text and deleted it. Maybe you decided the conversation could wait until morning. Maybe you took one breath before answering.

Write some of those moments down too. Then ask what helped. Sometimes it was the breath itself. Sometimes you suddenly remembered that the other person was exhausted. Maybe you pictured your child watching you or remembered a value you didn't want to violate. Sometimes you were simply too tired to argue. It all counts.

Each of those moments proves that the pause isn't a foreign skill you have to import into your life. You're already doing it. The work is learning how to bring that same capacity into the moments where your emotions are louder. You may also notice that your body already gives you natural speed bumps. Maybe your hand goes to your chest. Maybe you take a long exhale, pace, or step into the bathroom before returning to a difficult conversation. You may have thought of those things as nervous habits. They can become deliberate pause rituals instead.

The hand on your chest can become a reminder to take one real breath. The trip to the bathroom can become thirty seconds to feel your feet on the floor before you go back into the room. It also helps to notice where your steadier self shows up more easily. There are probably people around whom you think more clearly and places where you naturally feel calmer. Ask yourself what's different there. Maybe you feel safer. Maybe you know what to expect. Maybe nobody is rushing you.

You won't always be able to recreate those conditions in the hard moments, but you can often borrow one piece of them. A little more time. A slightly kinder assumption. One breath before you answer. Sometimes that's enough to change the turn.

Choose One Place to Begin

By now you'll have a lot of information, and the temptation will be to work on everything at once. Don't. Choose one of your three patterns, then choose one ordinary situation where it tends to show up. Make it something moderate. You don't want the easiest thing in your life, but you also don't want the issue that overwhelms you before you can think. Pick something that happens often enough to practice on and carries enough emotion that you'll know when the skill is working.

Starting small isn't avoiding the bigger things. It's training. You wouldn't learn to lift weights by starting with the heaviest thing in the gym. You build the muscle on something you can actually lift, then trust that the strength will be there when you need more of it.

Keep the map you made somewhere you can get to it. In the chapters ahead, when we begin using the pause in real time, in your body, your relationships, your boundaries, and your family, you'll keep coming back to the pattern you chose here. For now, the work is simply to see it clearly.

What felt like an ambush may turn out to be an intersection you've been passing through for years. Once you know where the intersection is, you can begin learning another way through it.

Chapter Four

Chapter 4: Practicing the Pause in Real Time

Everything so far has been preparation, and preparation matters, but it isn't where you actually live. You live in the moment when your phone lights up with that name, or your child gives you a flat "no" that lands like a slap, and you have maybe three seconds before your mouth or your thumbs are already moving. If the pause can't fit inside those three seconds, it won't help you much, because the moments that undo you rarely arrive when you have a worksheet nearby and twenty quiet minutes to think. This chapter is about what the pause looks like in real time, at real speed. The good news is that three seconds is longer than it feels. With a few small moves, you can stretch those seconds just enough to make a choice instead of getting dragged into the old reaction.

What the Pause Actually Is in the Moment

When I use the word pause, I don't mean something peaceful or meditative. You don't need a quiet room, a long breath, or a mind that suddenly goes blank. The pause I'm talking about is much smaller than that. It's a brief interruption in the automatic chain between what happens and what you do next. It might be one breath, one silent question, or a slow count to three.

You also don't have to feel calm before you use it. That matters, because a lot of people wait for calm before they try to respond differently, and calm rarely arrives on command. You can still be angry, anxious, hurt, or flooded and pause anyway. The goal is simply to slow the reaction by a fraction. Sometimes half a second is enough to change the words you choose, the tone you use, or whether you respond at all.

It also helps to know what a pause isn't. Swallowing what you feel and saying nothing isn't a pause. That's disconnection, and it often comes back later as resentment or a bigger blowup. Freezing in fear isn't a pause either. That's your nervous system shutting down, and it's happening to you rather than being chosen by you. Automatically soothing or pleasing someone just to make the tension disappear isn't a pause either. That's an old survival strategy doing what it has always done.

What makes a real pause different is that somewhere inside it there's awareness and choice. Even if the only choice you can make is, "I'm too activated to handle this well right now, and I'm going to come back to it later," that still counts. You noticed what was happening and chose your next move instead of letting the reaction choose it for you.

Once you're inside that small space, there are two questions that can help. The first is, What pain just landed? That turns your attention toward what actually hurt before your mind starts building a whole story around it. The second is, What suffering am I about to add? That turns you toward the part you can influence, the next layer you may be about to build on top of the pain.

You don't need to ask both questions every time, and you certainly don't need to phrase them perfectly. In a hard moment, the words may be as simple as, What hurt? or What am I about to make worse? Even one honest question can be enough to change what happens next.

On bad days, aim for a good-enough pause. Sometimes you'll catch yourself halfway through the sharp sentence instead of before it. Sometimes you'll notice the reaction an hour later. That still matters. Softening the second half of a sentence is better than finishing it at full force. Realizing afterward that the Pain Wheel turned is still the beginning of learning to see it sooner.

This isn't a skill you install once and then own forever. It's more like a muscle. It gets stronger through a lot of ordinary, imperfect repetitions, and the clumsy ones count too.

A Toolkit You Can Use in Ten Seconds

You don't need a dozen techniques. You need a few that are simple enough to remember when your thinking starts getting crowded. One useful practice is what I think of as name, notice, breathe. First, name what's happening in the simplest language you can. I'm triggered. I'm flooded. My wheel is spinning. Giving the state a name helps create a little distance from it. You stop being completely inside the reaction and become someone who can also observe it.

Next, notice one thing happening in your body. Maybe your jaw is tight, your chest is buzzing, or your hands are cold. Don't try to make the sensation go away. Just notice it. That small act of observation gives you another fraction of space. Then take one slower breath, especially on the exhale. You don't need five deep breaths or a whole breathing exercise. One deliberate breath is enough to tell your body that it doesn't have to keep accelerating.

Another tool is a short phrase you keep ready for moments like this. Something like, I have a choice. Or Slow is safe. Or Pause, then respond. The exact words matter less than the fact that they're familiar and easy to reach. You can put the phrase on your phone, write it somewhere you'll see it, or simply repeat it often enough when you're calm that it becomes available when you're not.

You can also use a small physical movement to bring yourself back into the present. Press your feet into the floor and actually feel the ground beneath you. Touch your fingertips together. Put a hand on your chest. These are small enough that nobody around you needs to know you're doing anything. They interrupt the story racing through your head and bring some of your attention back into your body.

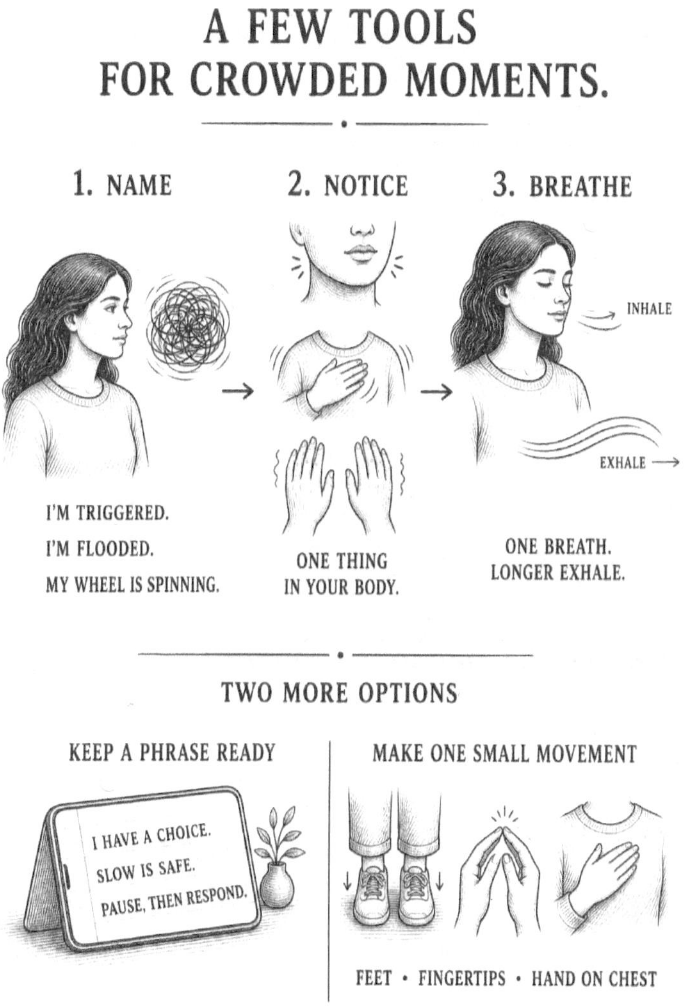
A FEW TOOLS
FOR CROWDED MOMENTS.
1. NAME
2. NOTICE
3. BREATHE
INHALE
EXHALE
I'M TRIGGERED.
I'M FLOODED.
MY WHEEL IS SPINNING.
ONE THING
IN YOUR BODY.
ONE BREATH.
LONGER EXHALE.
TWO MORE OPTIONS
KEEP A PHRASE READY
I HAVE A CHOICE.
SLOW IS SAFE.
PAUSE, THEN RESPOND.
MAKE ONE SMALL MOVEMENT
FEET • FINGERTIPS • HAND ON CHEST

Toolkit

Sometimes the best tool is simply saying out loud that you need more time. "Let me think about that for a minute." "I need a beat before I answer." "Can we come back to this tonight after the kids are down?" It helps to practice one or two of these lines ahead of time, so you don't have to invent them when you're already activated.

Some people worry that asking for time is avoidance or weakness. It isn't. Avoidance is disappearing from something you need to address. A deliberate delay is choosing to address it when you're more likely to do it well. That can save you from creating damage that takes days to repair.

Matching the Tool to the Moment

Not every reaction needs the same response. It helps to have a quick sense of how activated you are before you decide what to use. Think of it like a traffic light. Yellow is mild activation. You're irritated, uneasy, or a little off, but you can still think clearly. In yellow, you can use questions, reframing, or a delay line because most of your thinking is still available.

Orange is more intense. Your heart is going, the story in your head is getting loud, and you can feel the reaction getting ready to jump. This is where the simpler tools tend to work better. One breath. Feet on the floor. Your short phrase. The goal isn't to solve the whole problem. It's to keep the reaction from taking over.

Red is flooded. Your thinking is mostly offline, and trying to have a reasonable conversation at that point is usually a bad bargain. In red, the goal is to slow your body and create distance. This is the time to step away, delay the conversation, or do whatever safely helps you come down enough to think again.

Trying to use a subtle reframe when you're deep in red is like trying to read fine print while the fire alarm is going off. The tool has to match the state you're in.

Where you are matters too. Some pauses need to stay private. In a meeting or at a crowded table, you may only have room for a breath, a phrase in your head, or the feeling of your feet on the floor. At home with people you trust, you can make the pause visible. You can say you need a minute, step outside, or set a time to come back to the conversation.

Doing that in front of your children isn't weakness. It teaches them something important about what self-control actually looks like. They get to see that taking a pause doesn't mean running away. It means noticing when you need a moment before you make things worse.

The medium matters too. Texts and emails give you more room than live conversation. You can leave something in drafts, set the phone down, come back in an hour, or read your reply out loud before sending it. That last one catches an amazing amount of sharpness that your eyes will skim past.

In live conversation, silence and delay lines matter more. There's a big difference between saying, "Let me sit with that for a second," and going cold and silent. One is chosen. The other is the old wheel turning. Again, the difference is the presence of awareness and choice.

What It Looks Like in a Real Ten Seconds

Imagine it's Tuesday morning and your phone buzzes while you're making lunches. It's a text from your ex about the weekend schedule. The tone is clipped and just superior enough to hit the same nerve it always hits.

The old sequence happens fast. Heat climbs your neck. The thought appears: He thinks he gets to run everything. Your thumbs are already moving, and the reply you're about to send will probably buy you four days of cold, irritated logistics.

Now run the same moment with a pause inside it.

The phone buzzes. You feel the heat come up your neck, but this time you notice it. You recognize that you're in orange.

You're clearly activated, but you can still think. So instead of trying to talk yourself into some wise new perspective, you do something simpler. You put the phone face down. You press your feet into the kitchen floor and take one breath, letting the exhale run a little longer.

Then you say your phrase to yourself: Slow is safe.

Only after that do you pick up the phone again. This time, instead of asking who's right, you ask one question: What am I about to build here?

The answer becomes obvious. You're about to create four days of war over a scheduling detail that only needs a one-line reply.

So, you send the one line. Then you go back to making lunches. Maybe the whole thing takes fifteen seconds. Anyone watching would see nothing more dramatic than someone making sandwiches and checking a phone. But the war doesn't happen. That's the skill.

Notice what it didn't require. You didn't have to become calm. The heat was still there. You didn't have to like your ex or decide that the tone was fine. You didn't have to become a serene person. You noticed one signal, used a couple of tools you'd already chosen, and asked one honest question. That was enough.

Build Your Own Small Plan

The goal isn't to memorize everything in this chapter. If you try to carry a dozen tools into your next difficult moment, you'll probably end up using none of them.

Choose a small set. Pick one breathing practice you can remember, one short phrase, one physical move, and one sentence you can use when you need more time. Write those four somewhere easy to find, probably in your phone. That's your pause plan.

Four familiar tools will help you much more than forty good ideas you can't remember under pressure. When the next moment comes, you won't have to search through a mental catalog. You'll reach for the same small set you've practiced before. That repetition is what eventually changes the pause from something you understand into something you can actually do.

Chapter Five

Chapter 5: Changing the Story Inside the Pause

The first few times you manage to catch even a small pause; you may be surprised by what you find there. You might expect it to feel calm, like a little pocket of quiet between the trigger and your response. Most of the time, it doesn't. The pause can feel crowded. There may be several voices talking at once: Say something or she'll think you don't care. If you don't fix this right now, it's going to get worse. You always do this. The point isn't to make those voices disappear. It's to learn how to stand in the middle of them without automatically handing control to the loudest one. That's what turns a pause from a simple delay into a place where something different can actually happen.

Catch the Story Fast

When you're triggered, certain thoughts tend to arrive first and with unusual confidence. It's all my fault. They're so selfish. Nobody ever listens to me. They don't show up as possibilities. They arrive sounding like facts, and that's part of their power. A thought you never recognize as a thought is much easier to obey.

So, the first step is simply to hear the story clearly enough to recognize that it is a story. You don't have to argue with it yet. If you can catch yourself thinking, Nobody ever listens to me, and realize, There's that line again, you've already created a little distance from it. That distance matters because choice becomes possible there.

It can also help to notice the kind of thinking your mind is doing, not just the specific sentence it produced. Most of us have a few familiar moves. Catastrophizing takes one bad event and races straight to the worst outcome: I made one mistake, so I'm probably going to lose the job. Mind-reading decides what someone else is thinking without much evidence: He thinks I'm pathetic. All-or-nothing thinking gives you the world in always and never: You never help. I always ruin things.

Giving the pattern a name can take some of the force out of it. Instead of wrestling with whether the thought is true, you can notice, That's catastrophizing again. You're beginning to see the shape of the thought instead of getting carried away by the content.

A few stories seem to cost us more than others. One attacks your worth: Something is wrong with me. Another tells you that your feelings don't deserve room: I shouldn't feel this way. I'm too sensitive. Another talks you out of your own limits: It's easier if I just give in. Keeping the peace matters more than what I need. Most of us have a favorite. Pay attention to the one you hear most often, because that's probably the story worth practicing on first.

When you have the time, write the thought down exactly as it came. Put it in your phone or on the back of a receipt. Writing slows the thought down to the speed of your hand. Once it's outside your head and sitting in front of you, it becomes easier to examine. You won't always be able to do this in the moment, but when you can, it's useful practice because a thought on paper has a harder time pretending to be reality.

Ask Better Questions in the Gap

Once you've caught the story, the next step isn't to force yourself into positive thinking. It's to ask a better question than the frightened part of you is asking.

The first question is the one this book keeps coming back to: Is this the pain, or is this the suffering I'm about to add? Start by naming what actually hurts. Maybe the real pain is, I feel unimportant to him right now, and that hurts. Then notice what you're about to pile on top of it. The replay, the accusation, the verdict about yourself, the response that will make tomorrow harder. The question helps you find the seam between what happened to you and what you're about to do with it.

A second question is, What else could be true? You're not trying to invent a cheerful explanation you don't believe. You're only looking for another reasonable possibility. Maybe he isn't cold. Maybe he's exhausted. Maybe one mistake doesn't erase the ten things you handled well today. You don't have to be convinced by the alternative. It only has to remind you that the harshest interpretation isn't the only one available.

A third question looks a little farther down the road: What will I want to feel good about tomorrow? Imagine yourself twenty-four hours from now looking back at this moment. Which response would you be most at peace with? Sometimes you'll be glad you spoke up. Sometimes you'll be glad you kept quiet, stepped away, or chose kindness when something sharper was right there. Tomorrow-you often has better judgment than the version of you trying to decide in the next three seconds, so it can help to borrow that perspective.

The fourth question turns toward you: What's one kind thing I can offer myself right now? Maybe it's a hand on your chest. Maybe it's the sentence you would give a close friend in the same situation: This really is hard. Of course this hurts. Self-kindness may feel awkward at first, especially if you're much better at offering it to other people. But when you stop attacking yourself, you have more room to respond wisely to the person in front of you. You're no longer fighting two battles at once.

The Questions in One Ordinary Scene

Imagine you text a close friend with a piece of good news that matters to you, and she leaves the message on read for two days. By the second evening, your mind has started building a case:

She doesn't really care about me. I'm always more invested than everyone else. I'm too much, and people eventually get tired of me.

You probably know where that story leads. Maybe you send a wounded text. Maybe you say nothing and start pulling away. Either way, the friendship begins paying for a conclusion you haven't actually verified.

Now put a pause into the scene.

First ask, What's the actual pain? The answer may be simple: It hurts to feel unimportant to someone I care about. That pain is real. Naming it lets it be painful without turning it into a verdict on your whole life.

Then ask, What else could be true? Maybe she's overwhelmed. Maybe she read the message, meant to answer properly, and got pulled into something else. You've probably done the same thing to people you care about. You don't need to decide that this explanation is definitely true. You only need to admit that your first explanation isn't the only possibility.

Then ask what tomorrow-you would want to have done. Maybe the answer is to wait. Maybe it's to send a warm, direct message instead of a wounded one. And finally, offer yourself something kind: It's okay that I wanted her to respond. Wanting to matter to someone isn't a flaw.

None of that makes the sting disappear. It isn't supposed to. The pause simply keeps you from building several more layers of suffering on top of a two-day silence. Sometimes, as in this example, the ordinary explanation arrives the next morning in the form of an apologetic message about a brutal week. The pain was real. The rest didn't have to be built.

Speak from the Pause, Not from the Wheel

Eventually the pause has to shape what comes out of your mouth. The goal isn't only to feel differently inside. It's to let your words come from the steadier part of you instead of from the part that feels most threatened.

When you speak, try to describe your experience without turning it into a prosecution of the other person. Instead of, "You never listen to me," you might say, "When the phone comes out while I'm talking, I start feeling like what I'm saying doesn't matter." Instead of hiding your defensiveness behind an argument, you might simply say, "I can feel myself getting defensive right now."

The exact wording doesn't matter as much as the move. You're describing what's happening in you rather than announcing what's wrong with them.

The pause is also a good place to state what you need, and usually the shorter version is stronger. "I need twenty minutes before I can talk about this well." "I can't take that on this week." Long explanations often invite a negotiation you never meant to start. Sometimes they're also the old pleaser trying to earn permission for a limit that didn't need anyone's approval.

Sometimes the most regulated response is to say very little. If you're flooded, or the other person is clearly looking for a fight, trying to work everything out right then may only make things worse. You can say, "I'm not in a good place to talk about this well right now. I want to come back to it."

That kind of silence is different from going cold. One is chosen and protective. The other is the old pattern shutting the door. From the outside they may look similar, but inside they're completely different. One contains awareness and choice. The other doesn't.

When you miss the pause, because you will, repair is part of the same skill. You can come back and say, "I'm sorry I snapped at you. I was overwhelmed, but you didn't deserve that tone." You don't need a long defense or a full explanation. You're simply returning to the moment and handling it better than you did the first time.

That matters especially with children. They don't need to watch you get every moment right. They need to see that a person can lose the moment, recognize it, and come back honestly.

A Practice for This Chapter

This week, work with one costly story, preferably the one you hear most often. When it shows up, try to do three things. First, catch the thought and, if you can, name the kind of thinking behind it. Then ask one of the four questions, whichever one fits the moment. Finally, if you need to speak, try to say one sentence from the steadier part of you instead of from the Pain Wheel.

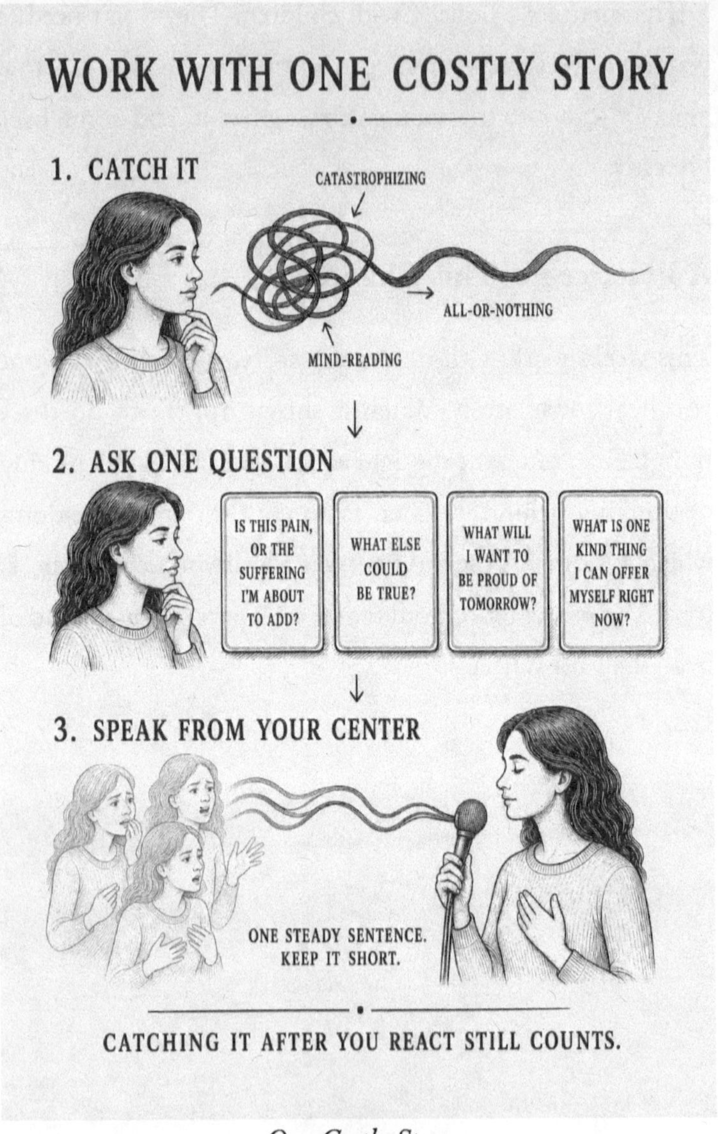

One Costly Story

You won't do all three perfectly. Some days you'll only catch the story after you've already reacted. That still counts. The goal is to become a little more familiar with the crowded room inside the pause and a little less likely to hand the microphone, every time, to whichever frightened voice happens to shout first.

Chapter Six

Chapter 6: Soothing Your Body in the Pause

There will be moments when your mind is saying all the right things. Breathe. You're okay. You have a choice. And your body won't listen. Your hands still shake. Your throat still tightens. You go numb, or the heat keeps climbing no matter how sensibly you talk to yourself. In those moments, the pause can't live only in your head because your head isn't where the problem is. The pause has to reach into your breathing, your muscles, and the older wiring of your nervous system. Learning how to settle your body isn't softness or self-indulgence. It's how you make the pause large enough to actually stand in when thinking clearly isn't enough.

Thinking Clearly Is a Luxury of Safety

There's a basic fact about how you're built that can save you a lot of unnecessary self-blame. When your body goes into high alarm, clear thinking becomes harder to access. That isn't a failure of discipline. Your nervous system has decided something is dangerous, and when that happens, it shifts resources toward survival. Your attention narrows. Your body prepares to fight or get away. The parts of you that plan, reason, and weigh options don't disappear, but they're no longer running the show.

That's why sensible advice can seem useless when you're flooded. You may know exactly what you should be telling yourself, and none of it seems to land. The problem isn't that you don't know better. The part of you that knows better is having trouble getting through.

Body-based tools give you a way back. They work underneath thought by using the language your nervous system already understands: breathing, movement, temperature, pressure, and sensation. The point isn't to avoid the feeling. It's to bring your body down far enough that you can feel what you're feeling without being overwhelmed by it and then return to the thinking and choosing the moment actually requires. Think of it as clearing enough smoke from the room that you can finally see again.

One helpful way to picture this is what's often called the window of tolerance. Imagine a middle zone where you can feel strongly and still think at the same time. Inside that window, you may be upset, angry, or anxious, but you're still present enough to choose. Move above the window and you become revved up, flooded, and overwhelmed. Drop below it and you may go numb, foggy, or strangely absent. The body tools in this chapter are meant to help you move back toward that middle zone. You're not trying to erase the feeling. You're trying to create enough room for the feeling and your wiser self to be present at the same time.

The first step is learning to notice what's happening in your body without immediately becoming frightened by it. If your heart is pounding or your stomach is tight, the alarmed part of you may interpret those sensations as proof that something is terribly wrong. Try describing them more simply. Tight. Buzzing. Heavy. Cold. Shaky. You're noticing the sensation without turning it into a verdict. That plain noticing is already part of the pause: Something is happening in me right now, and I'm going to stay with myself while it does.

A Few Tools That Work Almost Anywhere

You don't need a large collection of techniques. You need a few that work for your body and are simple enough to remember when you're activated. One of the most useful is breathing with a longer exhale. Breathe in gently through your nose for about four counts, then let the breath out slowly for six or eight. The exact numbers don't matter as much as making the exhale noticeably longer than the inhale. A longer exhale helps signal the body that it can begin slowing down. This can be especially useful when anger or anxiety is rising. Practice it when nothing is wrong, so it feels familiar when you actually need it.

Another tool is grounding through your senses. Look around and quietly notice five things you can see, four things you can feel, three things you can hear, two you can smell, and one you can taste. Don't get hung up on the count. The point is to bring your attention back into the room you're actually standing in instead of the catastrophe your mind is predicting or the scene it keeps replaying.

Temperature and movement can help too. Hold something cool. Splash water on your face. Step outside for a minute. Roll your shoulders, shake out your hands, or press your palms together and release. These small physical changes can interrupt the feeling of being trapped inside the reaction. They give your nervous system another message to work with: I can move. I'm here. This moment isn't as inescapable as it feels.

You may also find it helpful to prepare a few sensory things that settle you. It doesn't need to be elaborate. A smooth stone in your pocket. A scent you like. A photograph that steadies you. A short playlist that helps bring your system down. Keep something where you'll actually use it, maybe in the car, at your desk, or at home. The point isn't to create a ritual around calming yourself. It's simply to make support easy to reach when you need it.

Match the Tool to the State You're In

Not every tool works equally well in every state. The first question is whether your system has gone up or down. When you're revved up and close to exploding, the goal is to bring the intensity down. This is where the longer exhale helps. Movement can help discharge some of the energy. Cool water or fresh air can take the edge off. And if you're fully activated, delay the serious conversation. There's very little benefit in trying to settle something important while your whole body is at a boil.

Shutdown needs something different. If you're numb, foggy, or far away, more calming may only take you farther down. You may need gentle activation instead. Stand up. Stretch. Walk slowly around the room and name what you see. Hold a warm mug in both hands. Wrap yourself in a blanket and notice the warmth. The goal is to come back into your body, not quiet it further.

The middle zone is where you can do the most practice. When you're a little anxious or irritated but still functioning, use the breathing and grounding tools on purpose. Pair them with ordinary moments in your day. Take a few slower exhales at a red light. Notice your senses while washing dishes. If your body has practiced the route when the stakes are low, it's more likely to remember it when things get harder.

When the Body Has to Go First

Sometimes the mind tools simply aren't available, and the body has to lead. Picture the end of a long day. Something small goes wrong. A drink spills. Someone snaps at you. A bill shows up that you weren't expecting. Suddenly your hands are shaking, your chest is tight, and the words you usually reach for seem to be gone.

This is often the moment people turn against themselves. Why am I falling apart over this? Why can't I just handle it? But you're not necessarily falling apart. You may simply be outside your window, and trying to reason your way back in isn't going to work very well.

So don't start with reasoning. Hold a glass of cold water and notice the temperature against your fingers. Let your exhale run longer than your inhale several times. Step outside for a minute if you can. Run your wrists under cool water. Press your back against a wall and feel the pressure holding you there. You're not solving the problem yet. You're helping your body return to a state where solving it becomes possible.

That may take two minutes or twenty. The signal you're looking for is simple. The shaking begins to ease. Your breathing slows. Words come back. You can think in full sentences again. That's when the rest of the pause becomes available, the questions, the decisions, and whatever conversation still needs to happen. You didn't avoid the emotional work by tending to your body first. You made the emotional work possible.

This can feel counterintuitive, especially if you've spent your life pushing through with willpower. But when the body has taken over, more pushing usually makes the reaction worse. Going to the body first isn't giving up. It's often the shortest route back to the part of you that can choose.

Build a Small Body-Pause Plan

Keep this simple. Make yourself a short plan for the three basic states. When you're revved up, choose two or three things you'll try first. Maybe it's the longer exhale, cold water, and a sentence that gives you permission to delay the conversation. When you're shut down, choose a few things that bring you gently back, perhaps standing and stretching, holding something warm, and naming what you see around you. For the middle zone, choose one or two practices you can work into your ordinary day, so your body gets familiar with them before you need them under pressure.

Keep the plan somewhere you can find it. If there's someone you trust, it may help to tell them what you're practicing so they understand what you're doing when you step away or reach for one of these tools. Let the plan change as you learn yourself. What settles one person may irritate another. You're not trying to master the correct nervous-system technique. You're learning the particular body you actually live in.

The pause in the mind and the pause in the body are really two parts of the same skill. Some days your thinking will lead and your body will follow. Other days your hands will be shaking and the words won't come, and you'll have to begin with the body. Either way, the goal is the same: to find your way back to the place where choice becomes possible again.

Chapter Seven

Chapter 7: Using the Pause to Protect Your Boundaries

For years, you may have told yourself that the problem is that you just can't set boundaries. I think there's a kinder and more accurate way to understand it. If you watch yourself closely for a week, you'll probably discover that you do have boundaries. You feel them clearly. The trouble is that you often notice them a few seconds too late, after you've already stepped over them yourself.

You say yes while your body is quietly saying no. You stay in a conversation after everything in you wants to leave. You agree to help, then feel the resentment building almost immediately. The boundary was there the whole time. What was missing was a place to catch it before the old habit answered for you. That place is the pause, and boundary moments give you some of the best practice you'll ever get.

The Moment the Old Script Jumps In

Most boundary moments show up in the body before they become clear in the mind. Someone asks you for something, or an expectation lands on you, and before you've formed a thought, you feel a heaviness in your chest, a drop in your stomach, a flicker of dread, or the first edge of resentment. Those sensations aren't meaningless. They're early information that one of your limits may have just been touched.

If you can learn to notice that signal instead of pushing past it, you've found the doorway. Your body often knows a boundary moment has arrived several seconds before your mind catches up, and those seconds are exactly where the pause can help.

Without that pause, the old script usually gets there first. It's easier if I just say yes. She'll be hurt. He'll be angry. I'm being selfish. Good mothers don't say no. Good wives don't make things harder. Good daughters help.

Those thoughts come so quickly that they don't feel like thoughts at all. They feel like simple facts about what a decent person does. But they aren't facts. They're old lines you learned somewhere along the way, shaped by family, culture, experience, and whatever once taught you that keeping other people happy was safer than disappointing them.

When those scripts run unchecked, the behavior is predictable. You say yes and resent it all week. You stay late to solve a problem that was never really yours. You apologize for having a limit. You explain your no until it slowly turns back into a yes. Or you avoid the whole thing and disappear because you don't know how to say what you need.

Then comes the fallout: resentment, exhaustion, anger at yourself, and the feeling that once again you've let your own needs disappear. That becomes more pain, which makes the next boundary harder to hold. The Pain Wheel keeps turning.

So, begin treating the request itself as a checkpoint. You don't have to answer immediately. A simple sentence like, "Let me check and get back to you," or "I want to think about that before I say yes," can hold the gate long enough for you to consult yourself. Every time you pause before agreeing, you're teaching a system that has spent years answering automatically that it no longer has to do that.

Ask What You Actually Want and Need

Once you've created a little room, the first thing to consult is your body. Imagine saying yes and notice what happens. Then imagine saying no and notice that too. A yes that fits often feels clean, even if it means work. A yes that violates a limit tends to carry a different feeling: dread, constriction, or the sense of being tired before you've even begun.

That said, the body doesn't always give you a simple answer. If saying no once brought anger, rejection, or withdrawal from people you depended on, your body may still become frightened when no is exactly the right answer. So, listen to the body, but don't treat it as the final judge. Part of the work is learning the difference between the fear of an old consequence and the signal of a real present-day limit.

Then bring your values into the decision. Ask what matters most here. Honesty? Rest? Fairness? Being present with your children? Kindness that's freely given instead of resentfully performed? Fear asks, What choice will keep everyone from being upset with me? Your values ask, What choice fits the person I'm trying to become? Those questions don't always give the same answer.

This is where guilt often shows up. You say no, and suddenly you feel terrible. That can make you assume you've done something wrong. Guilt doesn't always mean wrongdoing. Sometimes it simply means you broke an old rule.

So, ask yourself, Do I feel guilty because I actually did something wrong, or because I did something new? From the inside, those feelings can be almost identical. In reality, they're very different. A healthy change can feel wrong for a while simply because your nervous system hasn't caught up with it yet. Keep the changes small. Burnout often produces dramatic boundaries: quitting, cutting someone off, declaring that everything is changing today. The pause usually gives you something more measured. You may not need to leave the committee. Maybe you take on less. You may not need to end the friendship. Maybe the calls become shorter.

Ten or twenty percent more aligned than last time is often enough. Small changes are easier to repeat, and repeated boundaries become much stronger than dramatic ones you can't sustain.

Speak the Boundary from the Pause

When it's time to say the boundary out loud, shorter is usually better.

"I'm not able to do that."

"That doesn't work for me, but here's what I can do."

"I need to say no this time."

The old pleaser will want to attach a paragraph. It will explain your schedule, your fatigue, your intentions, and all the reasons you hope will make the other person approve of your limit. Unfortunately, the explanation is often where the limit begins to dissolve. A clear boundary doesn't need a legal brief.

You should expect some pushback, especially if you're changing an arrangement that other people were comfortable with. Someone may be disappointed. They may ask again. They may tell you that you've changed. That doesn't automatically mean the boundary was wrong. It may simply mean they noticed that something really has changed.

You can hear their disappointment without surrendering the decision. "I understand that this is frustrating, and my answer is still no." You don't have to persuade them that your boundary is reasonable. You only have to keep it.

I still think the fence and leash distinction is one of the clearest ways to understand this. A boundary is a fence along your own property line, not a leash attached to another person. A fence says, "If the shouting continues, I'm going to leave the room." A leash says, "You're not allowed to shout."

The difference is wording and it's whose behavior you're trying to control. A boundary tells you what you'll do. It leaves the other person free to make their own choice, even when you don't like it. That's why a real boundary doesn't depend on their cooperation. It works the moment you follow through on your side.

Keep the pause available during the conversation too. If you feel yourself getting flooded while you're trying to hold the line, you can stop. "I'm getting overwhelmed, and I want to handle this well. I need a few minutes."

Then take the few minutes.

Stepping away long enough to regulate yourself isn't abandoning the boundary. It may be the very thing that allows you to hold it without turning the conversation into a fight. Expect to adjust as you learn. Some of your early boundaries may come out too hard because you've waited so long to set them. Others may be too soft because you're still afraid of taking up space. That's normal. You can go back and say, "I've thought about what I said, and I need to adjust it." This is what learning is all about even if it feels like inconsistency

Boundaries aren't monuments you carve once and defend forever. They're living lines that you keep tending as you learn what's true, what you can give, and what belongs on your side of the fence.

A Practice for This Chapter

This week, choose one small request you regularly say yes to even though you usually wish you hadn't. Before it comes up again, decide what sentence you'll use to create the pause. When the request arrives, don't answer immediately. Use the sentence.

Then give yourself thirty seconds and ask two questions: What happens in my body when I imagine saying yes and when I imagine saying no? And Which choice is more consistent with what I actually value? Then answer. Keep it short.

You're not trying to fix every boundary in your life this week. You're learning one much smaller thing: that there's enough room between a request and your answer to find out what you actually want before the old script decides for you.

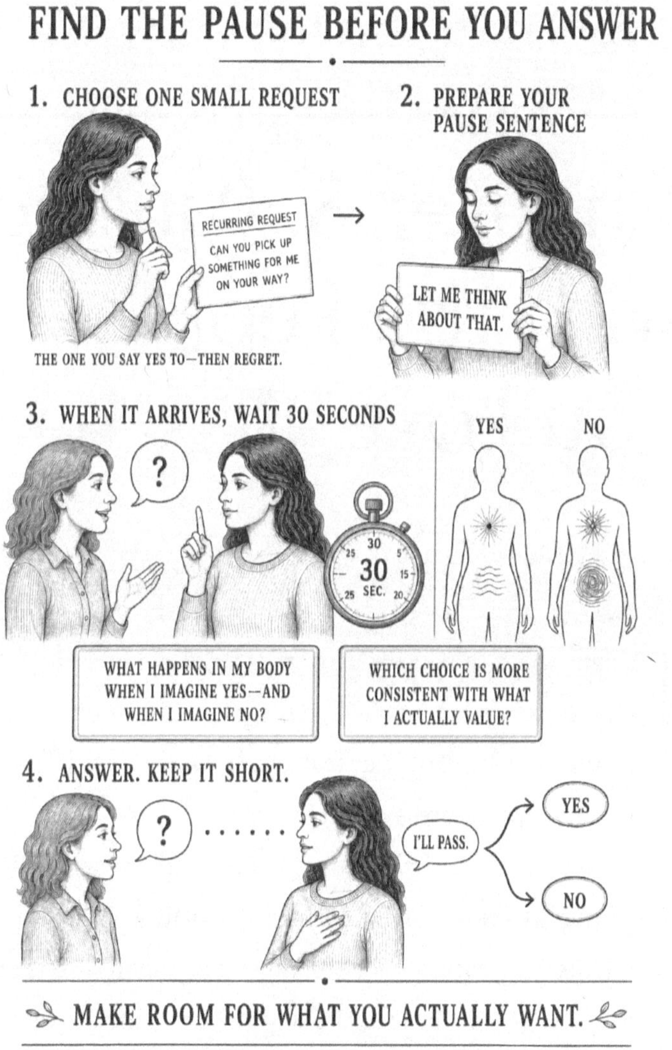

Pause Before You Answer

Chapter Eight

Chapter 8: Pausing with the People You Love

It's one thing to pause with a stranger in a grocery line. It's something else entirely when the person in front of you is your screaming toddler, your teenager behind a closed door, or your partner who knows exactly which words will land in the tenderest place. The closer the relationship, the faster the Pain Wheel tends to turn. Those are also the relationships where a small pause can matter most, because one different sentence can keep an old wound from being passed along to the next person. Home is where the work gets hardest, and where it counts the most.

Why It Is Harder Here

There are good reasons we often regulate ourselves better around strangers and coworkers than around the people we love most. Intimate relationships reach deeper. A partner, a child, or a parent can touch old attachment alarms in a way a casual acquaintance rarely can. Feeling ignored by a stranger may sting. Feeling ignored by your husband can drop you into something much older, because underneath all the adult reasoning, love and safety were once tied together. When one feels threatened, the other can feel threatened too.

There's also the simple fact that home usually gets what's left of us. By the end of a normal day, you've already spent energy making decisions, managing schedules, meeting needs, remembering details, and carrying a mental list that never quite closes. The same nervous system you're asking to pause at seven in the evening may have been working since before breakfast. So, when you discover that you have the least patience precisely when your family seems to need the most, that doesn't make you a hypocrite. It means you're working with a smaller battery. Knowing that lets you plan for it instead of turning it into another reason to judge yourself.

It also helps to let go of the imaginary person you've probably seen a thousand times on a screen, the endlessly patient mother or partner who moves through spilled milk, missed homework, and slammed doors with a calm smile. She isn't real. Healthy families aren't built by people who never lose their footing. They're built by people who notice when they do, repair what happened, and keep learning. The pause is meant to reduce unnecessary damage and make repair easier. It was never meant to turn you into someone who never gets rattled.

Remember that everyone in the room has a nervous system. Your partner has old alarms too. Your children are still developing theirs. A lot of ordinary conflict is two systems reacting at the same time, each convinced something important is at stake. That doesn't excuse harmful behavior, but it can help you see the moment more accurately. You don't have to decide who the villain is before you decide what to do with your own response.

Pausing as a Parent

Parenting puts all of this into very small windows. The milk spills when you're already late. Bedtime turns into another negotiation when you have nothing left. Your child asks one more question after you've answered twenty. Somewhere in those moments there's often a tiny physical signal before the reaction comes out. Your jaw tightens. Your voice starts to rise. Heat moves through your chest.

That signal can become your cue. One breath. One step backward. Sometimes that's all you have time for. Sometimes you won't catch it until you're already halfway through the yell. Catch it there. Lower your voice. Change the second half of the sentence. That's still a pause, and your child is learning something from watching you correct yourself in real time.

When you speak, try to separate the behavior from the child. "I'm angry, and I'm not going to yell." "That behavior isn't okay, and here's what happens next." You can be firm without turning the moment into a verdict on who your child is. That distinction matters. A bad choice is something a child can change. Being told that he is bad gives him something much heavier to carry.

The same principle applies when you miss the pause completely. Repair. "I'm sorry I shouted. That wasn't okay, and you didn't deserve that tone. I'm working on taking a breath before I react." That kind of apology doesn't weaken your authority. It teaches your child that people can get things wrong without pretending they didn't, that love survives a rupture, and that he is worth coming back to. Children who see repair learn that relationships don't have to be perfect to be safe.

None of this works very well if you are completely depleted. Caring for your own nervous system is part of parenting, not time stolen from it. Sometimes the most useful thing you can do is take thirty seconds behind a bathroom door, sit in the car for a minute before pickup, or ask someone else to carry part of the load while you come back to yourself.

Pausing with a Partner

With a partner, the challenge is different because the other person can answer back and usually knows exactly where the old sore spots are.

One of the most useful things to notice is the moment a conversation stops being about understanding and turns into a contest. You can often feel that shift. You're no longer listening because you want to know what the other person means. You're listening for the opening where you can make your case. That's a good place to pause and ask, What am I trying to prove right now?

The answer is often revealing. Maybe you're trying to prove that you were right, that you're not selfish, that the other person started it, or that your memory of what happened is the accurate one. But proving those things may have very little to do with what you actually want, which is usually to feel understood, respected, or close again.

Real listening is harder than waiting politely for your turn. It means staying with the other person long enough that you could describe their point in a way they would recognize as fair. That doesn't mean agreeing. You can understand exactly why your partner sees something differently and still hold your own position. But once someone feels genuinely understood, the temperature usually drops enough for an honest disagreement to become possible.

There will also be times when neither of you can do that well. When the conversation gets too hot, a deliberate time-out can protect the relationship. "I care about this, and I'm too activated to talk about it well right now. Can we come back to it in an hour?"

The return time matters. Walking away without saying when you'll come back can feel like abandonment or punishment. Naming the return tells the other person that you're not leaving the relationship. You're stepping away from the reaction.

When you do come back, speak from your own experience rather than building a case against theirs. "When you looked at your phone while I was talking, I felt my chest tighten, and my mind went straight to, You don't care what I'm saying." That gives your partner a view inside your Pain Wheel instead of putting them on trial. It creates a very different conversation from "You never listen to me."

There's one limit I want to state plainly. The pause is for the ordinary collisions of imperfect people trying to do better. It is not a tool for making abuse tolerable. If someone is being physically or emotionally harmed, the goal is not to become better regulated while the harm continues. Safety comes first, and that may require help from outside the relationship.

What Repair Sounds Like

Picture the end of a long week. Your eight-year-old has been needling his sister all evening. You've asked him to stop three times, and on the fourth, you lose it. Your voice comes down much harder than the situation called for, and you see his face change. He goes quiet.

The old pattern might be for both of you to retreat. You sit with the shame. He sits with whatever he made of the moment. Nobody says anything, and the incident simply becomes part of the weather in the house. Repair changes what happens next.

First, give yourself enough time to come down. Take the breath. Run cold water over your hands. Walk around for a minute. Don't try to repair while you're still defending yourself internally. Then go back. "I'm sorry I yelled. That was too much, and you didn't deserve that tone. I was worn out and I let it come out at you. That's mine. I'm working on handling that better."

Then stop. You don't need to grovel, and you don't need your child to make you feel better. You name what happened, take responsibility for your part, and let the relationship return to ordinary life. That small repair teaches more than a lecture could. It shows that loving people sometimes get things wrong, that wrongs can be named instead of hidden, and that your child is worth an apology. The rupture mattered. But it doesn't have to be the last word.

A Practice for This Chapter

This week, choose one relationship and one recurring hot spot inside it. If it's with a child, decide which physical signal you'll watch for in yourself and what you'll do when you notice it. Maybe your jaw tightens, and that becomes your cue for one breath before you speak.

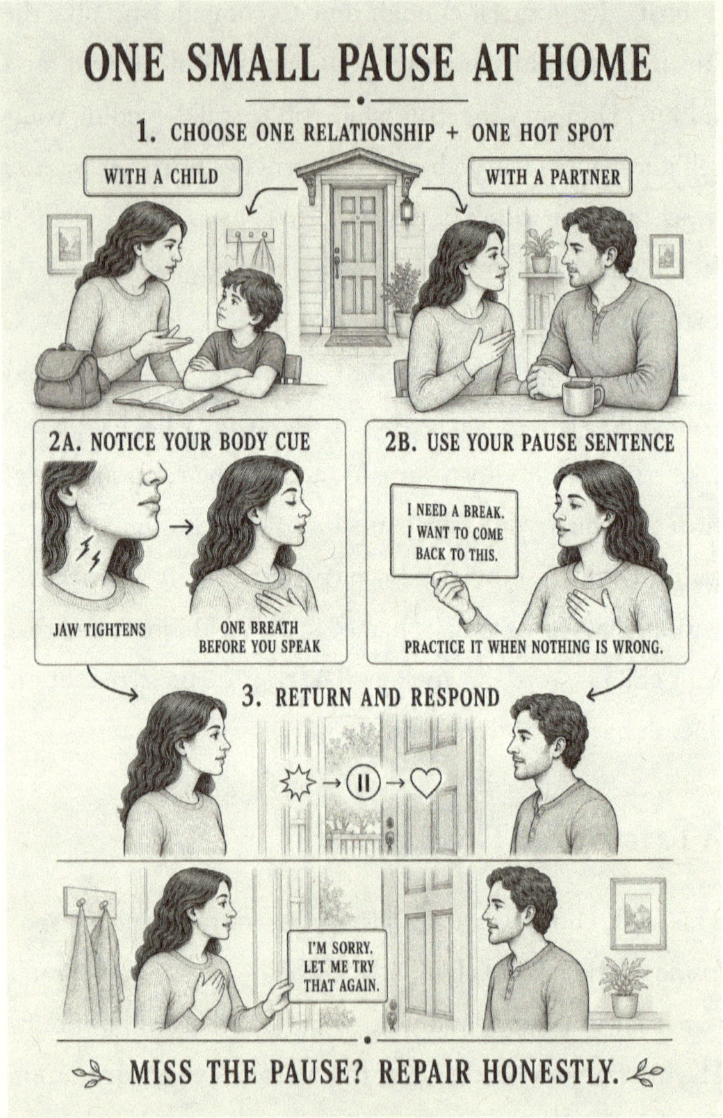

Pause at Home

If it's with a partner, choose one sentence you can use when the conversation moves beyond what you can handle well. Practice saying it when nothing is wrong, so the words are available when you need them.

You're not trying to become the perfectly calm person who never gets rattled. You're trying to bring one small pause into one familiar doorway of your home, then repair honestly when you miss it. In the relationships that matter most, that small change can carry a long way.

Chapter Nine

Chapter 9: Pausing Through Trauma Triggers and Old Wounds

Some moments don't just hurt. They pull you backward in time.

A smell, a slammed door, or a certain phrase said in a certain tone can do it. Suddenly you're not only standing in your kitchen in the present. Part of you is somewhere else too, back in a moment that ended years ago on the calendar but never fully ended in your body. Your system is reacting to both moments at once.

When that happens, telling yourself to calm down isn't very useful. It's a little like telling a firefighter to relax while the sirens are still going. When old trauma gets stirred up, the pause has to become gentler and slower than anything we've practiced so far. The goal isn't to force yourself back under control. It's to stay with yourself while the wave rises, moves through you, and eventually begins to pass.

Before we go any further, I want to be clear about what this chapter is and isn't. It can be a companion to trauma work, but it isn't treatment for trauma. If deep trauma runs through your life, you deserve a skilled person who can walk through it with you. My hope is that what follows can make that work a little steadier, not replace it.

Understanding Triggers Without Blaming Yourself

It helps to understand what's actually happening when you're triggered, because understanding creates room for compassion. A trigger happens when the past and the present begin to overlap. Think of a double exposure in an old photograph, where two images appear on top of each other. Something happening now resembles something that happened before, and your body reacts as though both are happening at once.

That's why the reaction can seem so much bigger than whatever is actually in front of you. Your system isn't responding only to the small thing happening now. It's also responding to the older thing that taught it what to fear.

Triggers are different for everyone. Raised voices do it for some people. Sudden movements, certain smells, anniversaries, or particular places do it for others. Sometimes it's the feeling of being trapped in a room or cornered in a conversation. Sometimes it's quieter than that. Criticism. Being ignored. Someone withdrawing affection. A familiar coldness in another person's voice.

As you think about your own triggers, pay attention to what happens in your body. Sometimes your body will identify the tender place faster than your mind will.

There's another piece of this that can save you a lot of shame. Willpower doesn't work especially well against a trigger, and that's not because you're weak. When your nervous system decides that an old danger has returned, it can move faster than your conscious intentions. Survival was never designed to wait around for a committee meeting.

So, you can know perfectly well that this isn't that and still feel your whole body react as though it is. Knowing better doesn't always stop a system that learned to protect you before you knew how to explain what was happening. In this territory, the pause isn't about commanding yourself to calm down. It's about respecting what your body is doing while trying not to add new suffering to an old wound.

Two things can be true at the same time. You aren't responsible for what happened to you, and you didn't choose the way your body learned to survive it. But you're still responsible for how you treat yourself and the people around you now.

Those truths don't cancel each other out. One gives you compassion for what happened. The other gives you power in the present. Responsibility isn't another way to blame yourself. It simply names the places where you still have some choice. The pause is where those two truths meet.

Trauma-Sensitive Pausing: Safety First

When trauma is involved, the definition of a successful pause has to change. Sometimes noticing, I'm triggered right now, is enough. You don't also have to become calm, say the perfect thing, and manage the moment beautifully. Awareness by itself may be the whole pause. If all you can do is shorten the wave a little or soften the edge of your reaction, that matters. You're practicing the skill under a much heavier load.

Use whatever grounding tool actually feels safe to you. That last part matters because not every calming practice works for every person. Some exercises ask you to focus closely on what's happening inside your body. For someone who's deeply triggered, that can sometimes make the alarm louder instead of quieter.

If turning inward feels like too much, start outside yourself. Look around the room and name what you see. Feel the weight of something solid in your hand. Notice the walls, the light, the furniture, the ordinary details that remind your nervous system that you're here, in this room, on this day.

Give yourself permission to stop any exercise that makes things worse. You don't owe a technique anything. Your sense of safety gets the final vote. It also helps to plan for triggers you already know about. If there are situations that reliably activate you, decide ahead of time what you'll do when one of them happens. Choose one or two gentle tools while you're calm rather than trying to invent them once the alarm is already going.

If you have a therapist, partner, or trusted friend who understands what you're working on, let them know the plan. A plan won't prevent every trigger, but it can change the experience from feeling completely ambushed to feeling at least somewhat prepared.

Don't overlook connection. Trauma tends to push people toward isolation, even though safe connection can be one of the quickest ways back. Identify one or two people you could reach out to when you're overwhelmed. Make the message simple enough that you don't have to compose it while you're struggling: I'm really triggered right now and could use a kind word. Reaching out isn't failure. Sometimes it's one of the wisest uses of the pause.

Bringing Compassion, Meaning, and Faith into the Pause

The way you speak to yourself during a trigger matters. Imagine someone you love sitting in front of you, shaking and overwhelmed. You wouldn't stand over her and explain everything she was doing wrong. You'd probably move closer, lower your voice, and remind her that she wasn't alone. Try offering yourself some of that same care.

Of course this feels hard. I'm here.

I'm not leaving myself alone in this.

That kind of language doesn't make the trigger disappear. What it can do is remove some of the shame that so often piles on top of it. Instead of turning the pause into another courtroom where you're on trial, you begin turning it into somewhere you can stand safely while the wave passes.

If faith is part of your life, the pause can also become a place where faith meets you. A brief prayer, a familiar line of Scripture, or simply the sense that you're being held by something larger than the moment can be grounding. Faith can also be misused here. Be careful about turning it into another way to scold yourself. If I really trusted God, I wouldn't be afraid. I shouldn't be angry. I should be over this by now. That doesn't comfort the frightened part of you. It gives it one more reason to feel defective.

If faith is going to help in a triggered moment, let it make room for what you actually feel. Reach for the parts of your faith that can hold grief, anger, fear, and confusion without demanding that you become fine before you're allowed to be loved. Meaning can come later too, if it comes at all. You don't have to decide that everything happened for a reason or that your pain was secretly a lesson. Sometimes those conclusions are offered too quickly and become another kind of wound.

A gentler question is, What does this reaction tell me about what matters to me? A trigger around abandonment may reveal how deeply you value being stayed with. A trigger around criticism may touch your longing to feel accepted or enough. Sometimes there isn't a lesson to extract. Sometimes the most honest meaning is simply this: That was hard, and I stayed with myself while it passed. That's enough.

Rest can be part of the pause too. After a strong trigger, you may not need another insight or another task. You may need quiet. A warm bath. A familiar show. Time outside. Something simple to do with your hands. Less demand for a while. If you've spent much of your life pushing through, over-functioning, and staying available no matter what your body was saying, rest can feel strangely irresponsible. It isn't. Sometimes rest is the clearest way to tell your body, This time, I'm not going to push you past your limits.

A Practice for This Chapter

Choose one trigger you already know well and make a small plan for it. Name the trigger plainly. Choose one grounding tool that actually feels safe, especially an outward-focused one if turning inward tends to make things worse. Identify one person you could contact and decide ahead of time what you might say. Then choose one compassionate sentence you can offer yourself when the wave comes.

Plan for the Trigger

Keep the whole plan small. You're not trying to conquer your triggers or reach a point where you never have them again. You're learning something more realistic and more useful: how to stay with yourself when one arrives, how to let it pass without abandoning yourself, and how to keep an old pain from becoming a new layer of suffering.

Chapter Ten

Chapter 10: Building a Life That Makes Pausing Easier

Up to now, we've treated the pause as something you use in the middle of a hard moment. But it can become something larger than that. It can become part of the way you move through your days. The choices you make about your calendar, your phone, your commitments, and even who gets your attention first all either create more room inside you or squeeze that room down before the difficult moment ever arrives.

You don't need to blow up your life and rebuild it from scratch to become less reactive. You need to begin shaping a life that gives your nervous system a little more room to breathe and gives the steadier part of you more chances to show up. The same difficult moment lands very differently on a woman who is rested and unhurried than it does on one who has been running on fumes for three days. A surprising amount of what looks like reactivity is decided long before the trigger arrives, in the ordinary structure of the week that came before it.

From a Skill You Perform to a Rhythm You Live

The pause becomes dependable the same way any other skill does: by practicing it when the stakes are low. Take a slower breath while you wait in a line that isn't moving fast enough. Notice what happens in your body while you read an email that mildly irritates you. Run through your senses while you're washing dishes. None of those moments is especially important on its own, but that's precisely why they're useful. You're practicing the pathway before you desperately need it.

Small repetitions matter more than occasional heroic efforts. They make the route familiar. When a real trigger comes, you're not asking your nervous system to learn something new in the middle of a storm. You're asking it to travel a road it has already been down many times.

It helps to attach the practice to things you already do so you don't have to rely on remembering. Take one deliberate breath when you start the car. Check your body while you brush your teeth. Let the sound of a notification remind you to put your feet on the floor before you pick up the phone. You can even set a gentle reminder that asks something simple like, Where's your wheel? or Feet on the floor.

These little habits become speed bumps built into the day. Without them, it's easy to move at full speed from breakfast to bedtime and then wonder why there's nothing left when the moment comes that actually requires patience. Your surroundings matter too. The environment you live in is quietly influencing how often your alarm gets pulled. You don't need to redesign the whole house, but you can make one or two places easier on your nervous system. Clear some clutter from the room where you tend to unravel. Create one small corner that feels settled to you, even if it's only a chair, a lamp, and a plant. Turn off notifications you don't need. Keep messages away from the dinner table. Stop letting the phone bring tomorrow's problems into the last hour before sleep.

There's no virtue in exposing yourself to more stimulation than necessary just so you can prove you can handle it. Every needless alarm you remove is one pause you don't have to perform. Keep track of the small wins. Not perfection, just evidence that something is changing. A one-line note at the end of the day is enough: I caught myself before I sent the text. I noticed the story even though I still snapped. I repaired sooner.

This kind of change can feel painfully slow from the inside because you're living through it one day at a time. But a few months later, you may look back and realize that something has shifted substantially. Keeping even a small record helps you see movement that discouragement would otherwise convince you never happened.

Expecting the Days You Fall Back

You're going to have setbacks. I want to say that plainly so the first one doesn't convince you that none of this worked. Growth rarely moves in a straight line. It's more like a spiral. You keep coming back to familiar situations, but you don't necessarily meet them from exactly the same place. Under enough stress, an old pattern may come roaring back and look almost identical to the way it did a year ago. That doesn't mean you've returned to the beginning.

Reaching for the tools again after a bad day isn't starting over. It's part of learning them. When you lose the pause, try doing a short review instead of putting yourself on trial. Ask three questions: What happened? Where did I lose the pause? And what did I do even slightly differently this time?

That last question matters. Your mind will want to skip it because it's easier to focus on everything that went wrong. But something is often different. Maybe you noticed sooner. Maybe you apologized the same evening instead of three days later. Maybe you rode the Pain Wheel twice instead of six times before you recognized it. That matters.

Keep the review brief. Once reflection turns into self-attack, you're not learning from the wheel anymore. You're riding it again. It also helps to plan for hard seasons before you're inside them. Some stretches of stress are predictable. Holidays. A major deadline. A sick parent. A period of heavy caregiving. If you know one is coming, decide in advance what one or two supports you're going to protect. Maybe sleep has to become nonnegotiable. Maybe you need the daily walk. Maybe there's one friend you need to stay in contact with because you know you become less steady when you isolate.

During those seasons, lower the number of things you expect yourself to do well. There may be weeks when maintaining a single pause practice is enough. That isn't lowering the standard. It's reading the conditions accurately.

When you feel as though you've lost your way, go back to the basics before hunting for a new solution. Notice the body. Separate pain from the suffering you're about to add. Take one slower breath. Look at the map you made earlier. The temptation is to assume that the old tools stopped working because the old chaos came back. Usually, they didn't stop working. You simply need to return to them. Musicians go back to scales for a reason.

What a Setback Actually Looks Like

Imagine you've had two good months. You've been catching the wheel more often, using your breath, repairing quickly, and starting to believe that maybe you really have changed.

Then life gets hard.

You haven't been sleeping. Money is tight. A parent is sick. One evening, something small happens and the whole old pattern comes back. You snap at everyone. You spin for hours. At three in the morning, you're replaying the same thoughts you thought you'd finally left behind.

Then comes the second wave: I haven't changed at all. I was fooling myself. I'm right back where I started. That second wave is the one I want you prepared for. You're not back where you started. If you look carefully, there will usually be evidence. This time you knew you were spinning. A year ago, you may not even have had language for what was happening. Maybe you recognized the pattern in the middle of it instead of days later. Maybe you'll repair in the morning instead of letting the tension sit for a week.

The old reaction can return while something in you has still changed. Heavy stress doesn't erase the work. It simply puts more weight on the system. The spiral can bring you close enough to an old view that you think you're standing in the same place, even though you're meeting it with tools you didn't have before.

So, when the setback comes, do the small review. Find the one thing that was different. Then return to the simplest practices and let them be enough for the season you're in. A hard stretch isn't the final exam on whether you changed. It's weather. Weather passes, and the practice will still be there when it does.

Growing With Other People

You were never meant to do all of this alone. The pause tends to take deeper root when there are a few people around you who know what you're practicing. You don't need a crowd. One person can be enough. A friend, a partner, a therapist, or a small group where it feels safe to tell the truth about both the progress and the failures. You might simply say, "I'm working on pausing before I react, and I'd like to be able to talk about how that's going."

Once two people share language for the wheel, the triggers, and the pause, they can begin helping each other recognize things that are hard to see alone. If you share what you're learning with other people, resist the urge to turn it into instruction. Ask before giving advice. "Do you want to hear what's helped me, or do you just need me to listen?" Tell your story instead of diagnosing theirs. Let people move at their own pace. The desire to force someone else to learn the thing that helped you can become another attempt to control something outside your line.

Often the strongest teaching happens without much talking anyway. Your children, coworkers, and friends notice when you stop halfway through a reaction, take a breath, and come back differently. A child who hears you say, "I'm getting reactive, so I'm going to take a minute before I answer," is learning something that many adults never learned.

That's how patterns begin to change across generations. Not because you lecture the next generation about emotional regulation, but because they watch someone practice it in front of them.

Before you close this book, decide what kind of relationship you want to have with the pause after the book is gone. It doesn't need to be complicated. Maybe it's one sentence: I'm going to keep looking for the gap and choosing one better response when I find it.

Check in with yourself occasionally. Once a month. Once a season. Look again at your patterns, your tools, and your values. Notice what has changed and where the old wheel still grabs you.

The pause isn't a project you complete. You'll lose it and find it again many times. Finding it again is part of the practice.

A Practice for This Chapter

This week, choose one anchor and one person. For the anchor, connect one pause practice to something you already do every day. Take one deliberate breath when you start the car or check

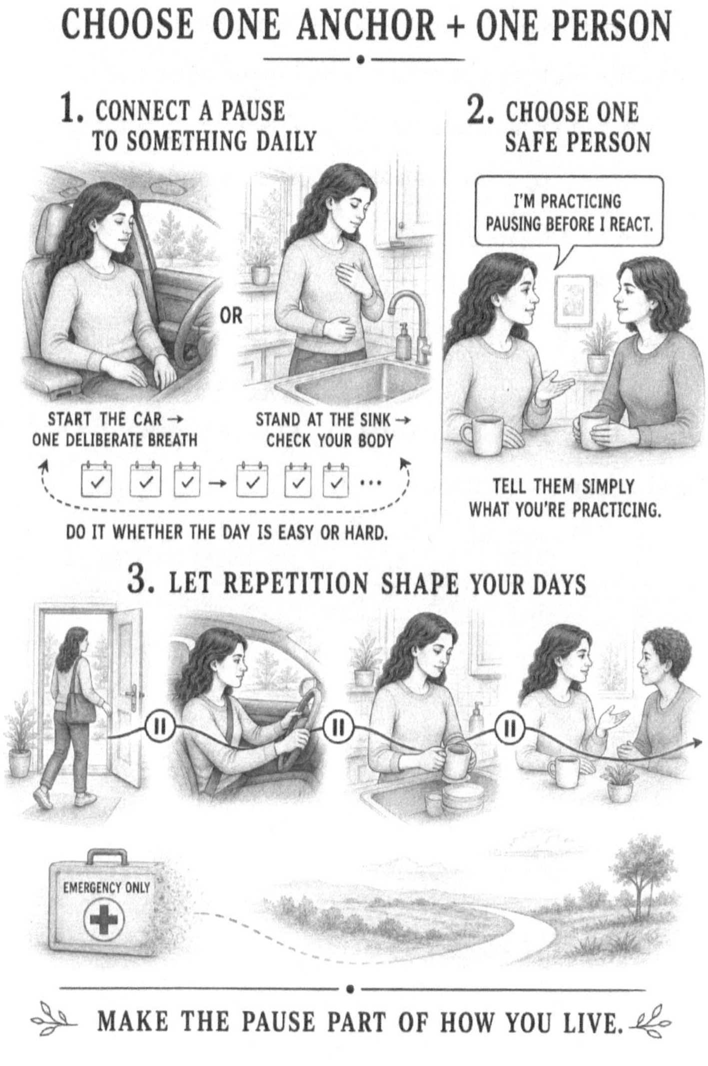

Keep Practicing

your body while you stand at the sink. Do it whether anything difficult happens or not. That's your repetition.

Then choose one safe person and tell them, simply, what you're practicing. You're no longer only learning how to pause once the storm has arrived. You're beginning to shape your days, your surroundings, and your relationships so that fewer storms have to be weathered at full force.

Over time, the pause can become less like an emergency tool you reach for when everything is going wrong and more like the ordinary way you move through your life.

Chapter Eleven

Conclusion: The Space Where the Mornings Change

We began at three in the morning, with you awake over a sentence, the soda-bottle pressure sitting in your chest, the replay running its loop. I want to end by returning you to that hour, because it is where you'll know whether any of this has taken root. Not in the calm afternoons, but there, in the dark, in the moment after the moment, when the old verdict comes to pass sentence on you again.

What has changed, if the practice has begun to work, may be quieter than you were hoping. You're not a different person. You didn't need to be. You're still sensitive, still deep, still someone who feels things fully and cares perhaps more than is comfortable, and I hope you never trade those away, because they were never the problem. What is different is smaller and stronger than a new personality. You've learned to find one small space, and to widen it, and to live in it a little longer than you used to. That is the whole of what this book set out to teach, and it is enough, because that one space is where every other change begins.

Look back at where you started. When you opened these pages, the moments that undid you felt like ambushes, arriving from nowhere, leaving you no say. Now you can name your Pain Wheel and feel it begin to turn. You can catch a body signal that used to slip past you. You have a handful of tools, a breath, a mantra, a question, a delay line, that live in your hands and not only on the page. Even if you use them clumsily, even if you use them half the time, you're no longer standing in the road with your eyes closed. You've seen the machinery, and a thing you can see is a thing you can begin to change.

Let me draw the whole map in a few strokes, so you can carry it out with you. Something happens, and it lands as pain, real and unchosen, in your body before your mind. Your mind rushes in with a story, and the story reaches for a verdict about you or about them. The Pain Wheel starts to spin, from pain to escape to a reaction that brings a moment of relief and then a consequence that drops you right back into the pain, a little heavier each turn. And there, at the top of the wheel, in the sliver between what happened and what you do, is the pause. Inside it live the only two things that were ever truly yours, your actions and your attitudes, what you do and how you hold what is happening. Everything else, the other person, the past, the outcome, sits on the far side of a line you cannot cross and were never meant to. The whole practice comes down to finding that sliver, again and again, and choosing from what is actually yours.

You will keep losing it. I want to leave you certain of that, so it cannot discourage you when it happens. There will be mornings you blow right past the gap and notice only at three a.m., and days the old pattern takes the wheel as if you had never read a word. Losing the pause does not erase the work. The noticing afterward, even when it comes far too late, is the muscle still firing, and the repair you make is not the booby prize for failing; it is part of the practice, and in the rooms you love most, it may be the best part. Treat every setback as the wheel showing you where it still grips hardest, so you know where to bring the next small pause.

If you forget everything else, keep a few things within reach. One breath with a long exhale, for the body. One question, is this the pain, or the suffering I'm about to add, for the mind. And one honest sentence, said from your center instead of your wheel, for the people in front of you. Those three will carry you through most of what an ordinary hard day can throw at you, and they fit in the ten seconds you'll actually have.

I do not want to leave you thinking this was only ever about managing yourself, because it was always about more than that. Every time you choose the pause instead of the wheel, you're protecting the things you most value, and you're doing something larger than your own peace. You're softening a pattern before it reaches your children. You're showing the people around you, without a single lecture, that a person can feel a great deal and still choose her response, that a big feeling does not have to become a big wound handed to the next person in line. The pause you build in your own kitchen can end at your feet a chain that has been running through families for generations. That is not a small thing to do with one breath.

I said at the beginning that I would come to this as a witness and not as an authority on your life, and I've tried to keep that promise, because you are the authority on your life, and you always were. What I've watched, sitting with people in their hardest seasons, is that the ones who change are almost never the ones who found some grand solution. They are the ones who got a little better at one ordinary moment, and then another, until the moments added up to a different way of being. And if you've made it this far, you've at least done one important thing: you've stopped long enough to look closely at the way you respond and ask whether there might be another way.

This small book was only ever meant to teach the one move. If it has done its work and you find yourself wanting the fuller picture, the whole framework the pause belongs to, the six practices that grow out of it and the deeper account of how these patterns form and finally break, that is what my larger book, Choose Your Response, is for. The pause is the first door. There's a good deal of house on the other side of it, and you're welcome in all of it whenever you're ready.

For now, though, let me send you back to three in the morning, one last time, with something you didn't have before. The next time you're awake over a sentence, with the pressure in your chest and the replay starting its loop, see if you can find the smallest gap inside even that, and offer yourself, in the dark, the one kind thing you would offer a frightened friend.

Of course this is hard. You're learning something new, late in a long night, and you're not alone in it. Then take one slow breath, let the morning come, and know that every new pause is a fresh place to begin. You've been awake long enough. The space you have been building is real, and it is yours, and it is where the mornings finally start to change.

Thank You

You made it to the last page. That matters more than you might think: most books get abandoned, and most patterns get kept. You stayed and now have the tools to reshape your patterns. I have additional free resources available. Follow the QR code below and I'll send you the packet.

However this book found you, thank you for letting me walk this stretch of the road with you.

Michael J. Rogers

About the Author

Michael J. Rogers, Ph.D., is a Licensed Mental Health Counselor-Qualified Supervisor, Board Certified Master's-Level Addictions Professional, Board Certified Sex-Offender Treatment Provider, and educator who has spent his career helping people uncover and break the patterns that keep them stuck. His clinical and forensic work spans the counseling room and the courtroom, centering on addiction, recovery, and the everyday struggles that follow people home: conflict, resentment, anxiety, and the stories we build on top of our pain. His doctoral research developed a cognitive reframing curriculum originally designed for an incarcerated population and later adapted for broad clinical treatment, testing whether people in the hardest circumstances can change their trajectory by changing their interpretations. The conviction that they can runs through every chapter of this book.

www.ingramcontent.com/pod-product-compliance
Lightning Source LLC
LaVergne TN
LVHW100148061126
851857LV00010B/291